Month-by-Month Poetry
December, January & February

Compiled by Marian Reiner

SCHOLASTIC
PROFESSIONAL BOOKS

NEW YORK • TORONTO • LONDON • AUCKLAND • SYDNEY
MEXICO CITY • NEW DELHI • HONG KONG

With love to Brian, who makes every Ground Hog Day special

Cover design by Jaime Lucero
Cover illustration by Amanda Haley
Interior design by Solutions by Design, Inc.
Interior Illustration James Graham Hale

ISBN: 0-590-37900-3

Contents

December

January

February

Introduction

Welcome to *Month-by-Month Poetry: December, January & February*. This seasonal collection offers more than 60 poems to combat the doldrums of winter and add sunshine, humor, and inspiration to your curriculum.

The perfect complement to winter's ways, poetry comforts, educates, and excites. Like music, it stirs the emotions and gives dimension to sights, sounds, and experiences. Poetry carefully woven lets readers hear the rustle of dry leaves in December and imagine a bear's dreams in hibernation. It enhances listening skills, builds literacy, and makes children eager to read.

First Day of Winter

Fall has fallen
Winter rises.
Now's the time
for cold surprises.

Icicles' long pointed noses,
Flakes like daisies, diamonds,
roses.
Snow up to the windowsill
And everything so very still.

—Patricia Hubbell

As you use and explore the poems in this book, you'll bring enchantment to life in your classroom—and reinforce concepts across the curriculum. Your students will celebrate holidays, personalize history, and grasp the essence of the winter season through imagery, rhythm, and rhyme. They'll explore emotions and rejoice in new beginnings, taste icicles, watch wildlife, and delight in the SPLIT-SPLAT of boots tromping through thick pools of slush.

The poems in this book are fun, easy, and appealing to students in the primary grades. They deal with such topics as winter weather, animal life, and a host of holidays from Hanukkah to Presidents' Day. For easy reference, we've divided the poems by the month in which they might be most useful. December poems deal with snow, gift-giving, and holiday traditions. January poems bring on new beginnings, winter colds, and hibernation. February poems focus on cold-weather animals, valentine sentiments, and the promise of spring.

The following activities offer some ideas for using these poems in your classroom. Launch the activities into action or use them as springboards for your own creative ideas. However you do it, rely on this resource to foster a strong love for poetry. Help students appreciate the beauty in poetry and capture its essence by reading it, playing with it, and writing it themselves. Be careful about asking students to dissect poems for meaning or to memorize them. Rather, set out to help them enjoy and experience poetry simply because it is pleasing. The rest will take care of itself.

Activities Ideas

TO FREEZE OR NOT TO FREEZE

Icicles freeze, but what about mustard? After reading the poem "Spirals of Silver," help your students conduct a classroom experiment to find out what freezes in the chilly North Wind besides water. Divide the class into groups of four or six. Provide each group with an empty ice-cube tray. On a table at the front of the room, place containers of liquids or foods that may or may not freeze, such as: fruit juice, mustard, mayonnaise, maple syrup, milk, olive oil, shredded cheese, soda, and cereal. Have each group fill its ice-cube tray with various items and make a chart to record the name of each item used. Place the trays in a freezer (or outdoors, if temperatures are below freezing) for several hours. Then have students record the results on their charts.

WHAT FREEZES?	
Item Used	**Did It Freeze?**
olive oil	no
water	yes
fruit juice	yes

Fill extra trays with water. When these freeze, give each student an ice cube to hold, taste, and melt in their hands for a dramatization of "Icicle."

SOLVE AN ANIMAL MYSTERY

Make your students instant detectives in winterland! Read "Who?" aloud, and invite your students to write and/or illustrate their responses to one of the questions posed or suggested in the poem. Who criss-crossed in fresh snow? How did Rabbit go away and why? What did the deer see, and what did she hear that caused her to run away? Who walked on two legs in the snow? Encourage students to use their imaginations, creating story lines beyond the basic poem. (They may write responses in poetry if they feel so inclined.) Copy "Who?" on a sheet of chart paper, post it on a bulletin board or wall, and display students' work around it.

EXPLORE METAPHOR

Help students understand that poets use metaphor to create an image or convey a point. In "December Leaves," for example, the poet likens fallen leaves on the lawn to cornflakes in a wide dish. Share the poem with your students. Invite them to circle examples of metaphor. Then have students illustrate their favorite metaphors in the poem, writing the appropriate part of the verse as a caption. Look for further examples of metaphor in "Friendship Time," "Winter in the School Yard," and "My Love Is Like a Cabbage." **HINT:** Let students give metaphor a real-life effect by gluing cornflakes and plastic spoons on paper and sprinkling with confectioner's sugar or baby powder.

WHAT ARE YOU DREAMING OF, BEAR?

Share "Grandpa Bear's Lullaby," and invite students to step into the bear's cave and imagine the dreams a sleeping bear might have. Students can illustrate and write/dictate their dreams. Compile their writing to make a class dream book. Then hang a dark sheet in a corner of the classroom, cover the floor inside it with pillows, and encourage students to use it as a cave in which to read the dream book during free time.

COUNT ON!

Let students count and write math word problems based on a poem such as "Presents." For example, a student might write, "Joe got a paddle ball, a jump rope, and a magnifying glass as gifts. He gave the paddle ball to Alicia. How many gifts does Joe have left?" Let students exchange math problems for classmates to solve. Younger students may simply want to write basic sums, such as:

1 picture book + 2 banks = 3 gifts.

Questions you might ask to prompt counting include: How many animals are mentioned in "Who?" How many gifts in "Presents"? How many items of clothing is the child wearing in "Winter Clothes"?

WHAT'S THE WEATHER LIKE?

Weather is a hot—or cold—topic in many winter poems. Move with your students through poetic tales of snow, sleet, ice, rain, and cloudy darkness. Then encourage them to recreate weather conditions on paper using a variety of art supplies, such as chalk (snow, fog, and clouds), clear glue (let dry in globs as raindrops), cotton (clouds or fog), or cellophane (icicles).

USE POEMS WITH POCKET CHARTS

Use a pocket chart to let students insert their own rhymes into a poem. Write each line of a poem on a separate strip of tagboard. Place the lines in order on the pocket chart, and read the poem aloud. Then use short strips of tagboard to cover the portions of the poem that rhyme. For example, the first two lines of "Good-bye My Winter Suit" read as follows:

Good-by my winter suit
Good-by my hat and boot,

In this case, cover the words "winter suit" and "hat and boot." Ask students to come up with their own rhymes to replace them. Write these on small strips of tagboard and place them in the poem. For example, students might write:

Good-by my mittens blue
Good-by my snowpants too.

When students have replaced every rhyme, read the poem aloud.

FOLLOW THE LEADER

Poetry and movement go hand-in-hand—especially when the poem outlines movements step-by-step! That is the case with the poem "Winter Angel," which tells students exactly how to move to create their own snow angel. Other poems, such as "Slush Song," inspire students to move as they see fit. Encourage movement in your classroom. Look for poems that invite or inspire movement, and move along as you read aloud.

FLANNEL BOARD FUN

Create your own snow person to go with the poem "Snow Woman." Using felt, cut out a snow woman, all of the clothing described in the poem, a carrot nose, a crescent moon, and a round sun. Then have your class sit in a circle around a flannel board. Place the snow woman on the flannel board, and distribute her clothing, the carrot, the moon, and the sun to your students. Read the poem aloud slowly. As you name each item in the poem, have the student who is holding it come up and place it on the snow woman or above her in the sky.

NOTE: While students are gathered together, take this opportunity to strengthen reading skills by copying the poem onto chart paper and pointing to the words as you read them aloud.

USE POEMS AS A SPRINGBOARD

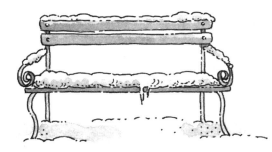

Use poetry to inspire student writing. Find poems that seem to have depth, interesting characters, or the hint of a storyline, such as "Snowy Benches" and "Joe." Invite students to write or dictate their own fiction stories based on the poems. Encourage them to illustrate their stories, and display them on a bulletin board or wall surrounding a large copy of the poem.

MAKE SHAPE BOOKS

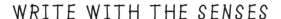

Cut paper in the shape of one animal featured in a poem, such as a bear, a penguin, or a squirrel. Give each student six sheets of paper stapled together to make a shape book. Ask students to write one fact about the animal on each page of the book. Students will find many facts in the poems themselves. You might also provide picture books, wildlife magazine articles, and other resources to use for fact-finding. Two poems rich in details for shape books are "Polar Bear" and "Emperor Penguins."

WRITE WITH THE SENSES

Use the five senses to write poetry with your students. Read aloud a sensory poem, such as "The Sound of Water" or "Chicken Pox." Invite your students to mimic the poem and—as a class or independently—write a similar poem describing the sights, sounds, or sensations of something familiar to them. They might list the sounds they hear in a lunchroom, on the school bus, or outside on the playground. Perhaps they'll describe how it feels to have a sore throat and stuffed head or how it feels to be sleepy and trying to stay awake.

LEARN MORE ABOUT HOLIDAYS

The winter season is packed with reasons to celebrate: Hanukkah, Christmas, Kwanzaa, New Year's, Valentine's Day, and more. Share related poems with your students. Invite them to tell what they know about the holidays they celebrate

with their families. Read picture books to help students hear about holidays they'd like to know more about. Invite people from the community to visit your classroom and bring stories, songs, and traditional holiday symbols to share with your students. Some of the holiday poems in this book include "Song of Hanukkah," "Merry Christmas," "Kwanzaa Time Is Here," and "Happy Chinese New Year."

SEND HOME A POEM!

Draw families into the poetry experience by sending poems home now and then. Attach a brief note asking families to use the poem together in some way and then sign and return it to you with a short description of how they used it. For example, you might:

◉ Send home a copy of "It Fell in the City." Ask families to take a walk outside their own homes and write down the items or landmarks that would turn white if covered with snow in their neighborhoods.

◉ Invite families to send in their favorite holiday poems or songs of Hanukkah, Christmas, or whatever winter holiday(s) they celebrate.

◉ Prior to the 100th day of school, send home a copy of the poem "Today Is the 100th Day of School," and ask each family to send in 100 pieces of food to contribute to a class "100 mix." Assign each family a specific food item, such as 100 goldfish crackers, 100 pretzels, or 100 raisins to make for an interesting and tasty mix. Have family members work together to count out the 100 items, seal them in a plastic bag, and send them to school. Invite students to pour their 100 pieces into a large bowl. Then mix and serve as a 100th day snack!

First Day of Winter

Fall has fallen
Winter rises.
Now's the time
for cold surprises.

Icicles' long pointed noses,
Flakes like daisies, diamonds, roses.
Snow up to the windowsill
And everything so very *still*.

Patricia Hubbell

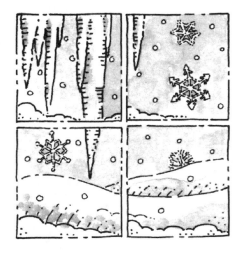

Winter Rhyme

Red boots
Blue boots
Green boots
Yellow

Sit by the fire
Pears are mellow

Trudge through the snow
Tramp it deep

Leap into bed
Curl asleep

Patricia Hubbell

December Leaves

The fallen leaves are cornflakes
That fill the lawn's wide dish.
And night and noon
The wind's a spoon
That stirs them with a swish,

The sky's a silver sifter
A-sifting white and slow,
That gently shakes
On crisp brown flakes
The sugar known as snow

Kaye Starbird

Month-by-Month Poetry: December, January, February   Scholastic Professional Books, 1999

Friendship Time

"Summertime is sparklers!"
  "Dandelion down!"
"Lions in the circus!"
  "Hydrants in the town!"

"Wintertime is popcorn!"
  "Snowflakes in the air!"
"Ice on every lake and pond!"
  "Gifts to share!"

"Summertime is friendship time!"
  "Wintertime is, too!"
"*Anytime* is friendship time—"
  "ME with YOU!"

  Patricia Hubbell

Who?

Who's been
criss-
crossing
this fresh snow?

Well, Rabbit was here.
How did he go?
Hop-hopping.
Stopping.
Hopping away.

A deer
stood near
this tall young tree.
Took three steps.
(What did she see?)
Didn't stay.
(What did she hear?)

Fox brushed snow dust
from a bush.
But who—
WHO
walked on TWO legs
here
today?

Lilian Moore

I Heard a Bird Sing

I heard a bird sing
   In the dark of December
A magical thing
   And sweet to remember.

"We are nearer to Spring
   Than we were in September,"
I heard a bird sing
   In the dark of December.

Oliver Herford

New Sounds

New sounds to
walk on
today,

dry
leaves
talking
in hoarse
whispers
under bare trees.

Lilian Moore

It Fell in the City

It fell in the city,
It fell through the night,
And the black rooftops
All turned white.

Red fire hydrants
All turned white.
Blue police cars
All turned white.

Green garbage cans
All turned white.
Gray sidewalks
All turned white.

Yellow No Parking signs
All turned white
When it fell in the city
All through the night.

Eve Merriam

My Nose

It doesn't breathe;
It doesn't smell;
It doesn't feel
So very well.

I am discouraged
With my nose:
The only thing it
Does is blows.

Dorothy Aldis

Winter in the School Yard

The yard is like a freezer.
We huddle in a bunch
and wish that we were all inside
eating steamy lunch.

We're standing still as statues.
We move to stir our bones.
But when we walk we feel as if
we're stiff as saxophones.

We'd rather be in music
singing loud as lions,
or painting at the easels,
spring things like dandelions.

Sandra Liatsos

Song of Hanukkah

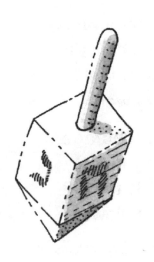

Come and sing a Hanukkah song.
Sing of heroes, brave and strong—
Maccabeus and his band,
Who rescued Israel's ancient land.

Sing a song of candles burning,
Dreidel spinning, pancakes turning,
Hanukkah presents tucked away
To open on the holiday.

Sing a happy Hanukkah song
Every day for eight days long.

Eva Grant

Hanukkah Rainbow

Eight little candles in a row,
Gaily colored,
All aglow.
Scarlet, purple,
Green, white, blue,
Pink and yellow,
Orange too.
The menorah,
Shining bright,
Holds a rainbow
Hanukkah night.

Eva Grant

The Twenty-Fourth of December

The clock ticks slowly, slowly in the hall,
And slower and more slow the long hours crawl;
It seems as though today
Would never pass away;
The clock ticks slowly, s-l-o-w-l-y in the hall.

Anonymous

Merry Christmas

I saw on the snow
when I tried my skis
the track of a mouse
beside some trees.

Before he tunneled
to reach his house
he wrote "Merry Christmas"
in white, in mouse.

Aileen Fisher

Kwanzaa Time Is Here

"Habari gani!"—What's the news?
What's the great occasion?
Let's pull together—"Harambee!"
To make a celebration.
It's Kwanzaa!
Time for Unity
and Self-Determination!
We'll share Responsibility,
and show Cooperation.
It's Kwanzaa!
Time for Purpose,
Time for Creativity,
and Kwanzaa's also time for Faith.
It's Kwanzaa! Harambee!

Helen H. Moore

Presents

My friends all gave me presents.

I got a gyroscope,
  some bubble bath,
  a paddle ball,
  a singing jumping rope,
  some finger paints,
  some paper dolls,
  a magnifying glass,
  a Fuzzy Felt Safari game,
  a swan spun out of glass,
  a picture book,
  a Teddy bear,
  a pencil,
  and two banks,
  and stationery with my name
  to send my friends my thanks—

  Myra Cohn Livingston

Surprises

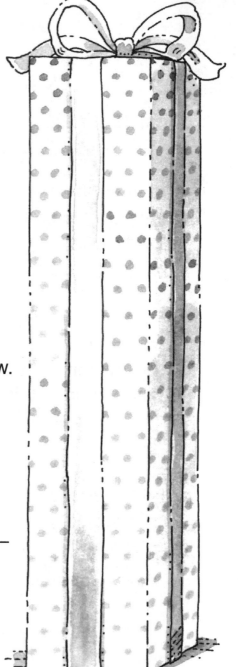

Surprises are round
   Or long and tallish.
Surprises are square
   Or flat and smallish.

Surprises are wrapped
   With paper and bow,
And hidden in closets
   Where secrets won't show.

Surprises are often
   Good things to eat;
A get-well toy or
   A birthday treat.

Surprises come
   In such interesting sizes—
I LIKE
   SURPRISES!

Jean Conder Soule

Month-by-Month Poetry: December, January, February Scholastic Professional Books, 1999

Bouquet of Roses

A bouquet of roses,
A bouquet of roses,
From this flowering bush;
Hark! The New Year's coming
And the old one's gone.

Olive tree, I'm leaving,
Olive tree, I'm leaving,
For the olive grove;
Hark! The New Year's coming
And the old one's gone.

Traditional Puerto Rican Song

Traigo un Ramillete

Traigo un ramillete,
traigo un ramillete
de un lindo rosal,
un año que viene
y otro que se va.

Vengo del olivo,
vengo del olivo,
voy pa'l olivar
un año que viene
y otro que se va.

Winter Angel

make an angel
in your yard
it isn't very hard

drop
like a fallen angel
into the snow

on your back
arms and legs
in a flap

stand
and your angel
stays
trapped in the snow

Monica Kulling

That Cheerful Snowman

That cheerful snowman
Guarding our door
Never will
See our daffodils.

Hannah Lyons Johnson

Lullaby for January

O little new month
your song is new
your song is ice
and snow and blue

O little new month
I love you so
I'll sing you to sleep
I'll sing you hello

I'll rock your cradle
I'll tell you a tale
I'll bring you a box
for your brand-new days
your brand-new days of dreams.

Patricia Hubbell

The Bell Hill

Out of the doors
our feet dash the red ground.
There is a sound
    like ringing
    as we touch down.

    It is New Year New Year
        New Year
    All around
        We hear the voices
        of greeting cheer
        in the warm South.

On the radio
the weather forecaster
speaks of ice and snow.
On television
the children of the North
dress full cover and walk the glistening ice.
What a show!

    It is New Year New Year
        New Year
    Far away and near
    there is joy in the warm South.

Birds in the yellow sun sing and we sing
        our voices ring
        over Bell Hill
        over the red clay:

  It is New Year New Year
  New Year
        It is New Year's Day!

Julia Fields

Happy Chinese New Year

"Gung Hay Fat Choy!"
In China, every girl and boy
celebrates the New Year
in a very special way—
With fireworks and dragons
colored red and gold—
They welcome in the new year
and chase away the old!

Helen H. Moore

Chinese New Year

Flowers and *Nin Wah*,
Tangerines, oranges,
Wealth and good fortune
   and luck to us all!

Midnight will bring us
Red envelopes, *Lai-See*,
Filled with some money
   and riches for all!

Time for remembering
Grandparents, parents,
Neighbors and friends:
   with fine gifts for them all!

We will be offered
a tray of togetherness,
Seeds, candied coconut,
   sweetmeats for all!

Days of the Dragon Play,
Nights filled with singing,
Then comes *Ten Chieh*
   with lanterns for all!

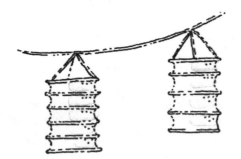

Soon the parade starts—
With loud firecrackers!—
the dragon is here!—
   Happy New Year to all!

Myra Cohn Livingston

Month-by-Month Poetry: December, January, February Scholastic Professional Books, 1999

Sound of Water

The sound of water is:
Rain,
 Lap,
  Fold,
   Slap,
    Gurgle,
     Splash,
      Churn,
       Crash,
        Murmur,
         Pour,
          Ripple,
           Roar,
            Plunge,
             Drip,
              Spout,
               Slip,
                Sprinkle,
                 Flow,
                  Ice,
                   Snow.

Mary O'Neill

Spirals of Silver

Silvery icicles—sharp and brittle
   March 'round the roof-edge, big and little
   One thin spiral curves at the end
   Because chilly North Wind made it bend

No two are alike as they sparkle and shine
   In icy perfection—a dazzling design
   In winter's white cold, they've nothing to fear
   'Til warm, sunny days when they'll all disappear!

Lorraine M. Halli

Icicle

Icicle is the strangest
Fruit from fairyland
   It tastes like—nothing!
   It goes to nothing
   In my hand.

Charlotte Mann

Month-by-Month Poetry: December, January, February Scholastic Professional Books, 1999

The Owl, the Snake, the Grouch, and the Children Greet the Snow

"Snoooooooooooooooowwwwwwwwwww!"
        hoots Owl,

"SSSSSSSSSSSSSSSSSSSSSSSSS NO!"
        hisses Snake,

"S NO NO NO NO NO NO NO NO NO!"
        grumbles Grouch,

But,
"SNOW! SNOW! SNOW! SNOW! SNOW! O! O! O! O! O!
    NOW! NOW! NOW! NOW! NOW!
        WOW! WOW! WOW! WOW"
            shout the Children.

Patricia Hubbell

Winter Clothes

Under my hood I have a hat
And under that
My hair is flat.
Under my coat
My sweater's blue,
My sweater's red.
I'm wearing two.
My muffler muffles to my chin
And round my neck
And then tucks in.
My gloves were knitted
By my aunts.
I've mittens too
And pants
And pants
And boots
And shoes
With socks inside.
The boots are rubber, red and wide.
And when I walk
I must not fall
Because I can't get up at all.

Karla Kuskin

Snowy Benches

Do parks get lonely
in winter, perhaps,
when benches have only
snow on their laps?

Aileen Fisher

Grandpa Bear's Lullaby

The night is long
But fur is deep.
You will be warm
In winter sleep.

The food is gone
But dreams are sweet
And they will be
Your winter meat.

The cave is dark
But dreams are bright
And they will serve
As winter light.

Sleep, my little cubs, sleep.

Jane Yolen

Flu

I'm wheezing
I'm sneezing

I'm coughing
    so loud.

I'm sputtering
I'm muttering
My head's in
    a cloud.

They say it's a fever,
They say it's the flu.
They say it's mysterious.
I say, "Ah…ah…CHOO!"

Terry Cooper

Chicken Pox

I've got the
itchy
itchy
scratchy
scritchy
head-to-socks
drive-me-crazy
Chicken Pox

Terry Cooper

Month-by-Month Poetry: December, January, February   Scholastic Professional Books, 1999

Bears

Bears
have few cares.
When the wind blows cold and the snow drifts deep
they sleep and sleep and sleep and sleep.

Elizabeth Coatsworth

Polar Bear

The Polar Bear never makes his bed;
He sleeps on a cake of ice instead.
He has no blanket, no quilt, no sheet
Except the rain and snow and sleet.
He drifts about on a white ice floe
While cold winds howl and blizzards blow
And the temperature drops to forty below.
The Polar Bear never makes his bed;
The blanket he pulls up over his head
Is lined with soft and feathery snow.
If ever he rose and turned on the light,
He would find a world of bathtub white,
And icebergs floating through the night.

William Jay Smith

Martin Luther King

Got me a special place
For Martin Luther King.
His picture on the wall
Makes me sing.

I look at it for a long time
And think of some
Real good ways
We will overcome.

Myra Cohn Livingston

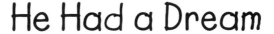

He Had a Dream

CHORUS:
"I have a dream!"
"I have a dream!"
These were the words
Of Martin Luther King.
What was his dream?
What was his dream?
Tell us the dream
Of Martin Luther King.

Dr. King wished,
Dr. King prayed
That one day all people
Would live unafraid.
Dr. King cared
For blacks and for whites.
He wanted all people
To share equal rights.

CHORUS

Dr. King marched,
Dr. King spoke
Of a world full of justice
For all kinds of folk.
Dr. King cared
For me and for you.
By working together,
His dream can come true!

CHORUS

Meish Goldish

Snow Woman

Snow woman snow woman
What do you know?
You sit so still
And silent in the snow.

Snow woman snow woman
Do you like your hat?
You sit so quiet
And comfortable and fat.

Snow woman snow woman
Do you like your clothes?
Your apron and your mittens
And your big carrot nose?

Snow woman snow woman
Sitting in the night
Does the dark scare you
Or the cold moonlight?

Snow woman snow woman
Here comes the sun
Are you afraid of melting
And being all done?

Nancy Dingman Watson

Month-by-Month Poetry: December, January, February   Scholastic Professional Books, 1999

Snow Stars

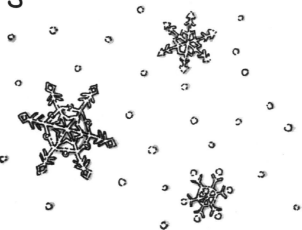

Delicate
And feathery,
Crystal clear
And white,
Six-point stars
Come tumbling,
Softly
In the night.

Regina Sauro

Joe

We feed the birds in winter,
And outside in the snow
We have a tray of many seeds
For many birds of many breeds
And one gray squirrel named Joe.
   But Joe comes early,
   Joe comes late,
   And all the birds
   Must stand and wait.
And waiting there for Joe to go
Is pretty cold work in the snow.

David McCord

January Thaw

Puddles dry up,
kites fly up.

Gloves off,
mufflers doff.

Pedestrians out,
smiles sprout.

No need to wait
until July:

pass your plate now
for more sky pie.

Eve Merriam

Month-by-Month Poetry: December, January, February Scholastic Professional Books, 1999

When

In February there are days,
Blue, and nearly warm,
When horses switch their tails and ducks
Go quacking through the farm.
When everything turns round to feel
The sun upon its back—
When winter lifts a little bit
And spring peeks through the crack.

Dorothy Aldis

Winter Wise

Walk fast in snow, in frost walk slow,
And still as you go tread on your toe;
When frost and snow are both together,
Sit by the fire, and spare shoe leather.

Traditional

Snow Animal

He tumbles in
And rolls around
Where the snow is deep.
I laugh because
He was my dog
But now he is a sheep.

Sandra Liatsos

Furry Bear

If I were a bear
    And a big bear too,
I shouldn't much care
    If it froze or snew;
I shouldn't much mind
    If it snowed or friz—
I'd be all fur-lined
    With a coat like his!

For I'd have fur boots
    And a brown fur wrap,
And brown fur knickers
    And a big fur cap.
I'd have a fur muffle-ruff
    To cover my jaws,
And brown fur mittens
    On my big brown paws.
With a big brown furry-down
    Up to my head,
I'd sleep all the winter
    In a big fur bed.

A. A. Milne

Waiting

Dreaming of honeycombs to share
With her small cubs, a mother bear
Sleeps in a snug and snowy lair.

Bees in their drowsy, drifted hive
Sip hoarded honey to survive
Until the flowers come alive.

Sleeping beneath the deep snow
Seeds of honeyed flowers know
When it is time to wake and grow.

Harry Behn

Month-by-Month Poetry: December, January, February Scholastic Professional Books, 1999

Consider the Penguin

Consider the Penguin.
He's smart as can be—
Dressed in his dinner clothes
Permanently.
You never can tell
When you see him about,
If he's just coming in
Or just going out!

Lucy W. Rhu

Emperor Penguins

Huddled close together
Against the snow and sleet,
Penguins at the pole
Pool their body heat.

They gather in a circle,
Steadfast, disciplined,
Turning toward the center,
Fighting off the wind.

Sharing warmth and comfort
On cold and icy floes,
Balancing their future
Gently, on their toes.

Barry Louis Polisar

Ground Hog Day

Ground Hog sleeps
All winter
Snug in his fur,
Dreams
Green dreams of
Grassy shoots,
Of nicely newly nibbly
Roots—
Ah, he starts to
Stir.
With drowsy
Stare
Looks from his burrow
Out on fields of
Snow.
What's there?
Oh no.
His shadow. Oh,
How sad!
Six more
Wintry
Weeks
To go.

Lilian Moore

Today Is the 100th Day of School!

(sung to the tune "The Ants Go Marching One-by-One")

We've all been counting one-by-one,
Hoorah! Hoorah!
We've all been counting, oh what fun!
Hoorah! Hoorah!
We've all been counting one-by-one,
And now 100 days are done,
Hooray! Today's the 100th day of school!

We started counting up to 10,
Hoorah! Hoorah!
To 20, 30, 40 then,
Hoorah! Hoorah
To 50, 60, 70 then,
To 80, 90, and now is when
Hooray! Today's the 100th day of school!

We started with a number low,
Hoorah! Hoorah!
And one by one, we made it grow,
Hoorah! Hoorah!
We started with a number low,
And now it's grown to 1-0-0,
Hooray! Today's the 100th day of school!

We've all been counting one-by-one,
Hoorah! Hoorah!
We've all been counting, oh what fun!
Hoorah! Hoorah!
We've all been counting, one-by-one,
and now 100 days are done,
Hooray! Today's the 100th day of school!

Meish Goldish

100 Is a Lot!

100 dogs, 100 cats,
100 heads for 100 hats.
100 women, 100 men,
100's more than 5 or 10.
100 buttons, 100 coats,
100 sails for 100 boats.
100 cookies, 100 cakes,
100 kids with bellyaches!
100 shoes, 100 socks
100 keys for 100 locks.
100 puddles mighty dirty,
100's even more than 30.
100 daughters, 100 sons,
100 franks on 100 buns.
100 trees, 100 plants,
100 picnics, 100 ants!
100 is a lot to count.
100 is a LARGE AMOUNT!
100 kisses, 100 hugs,
100 bats, 100 bugs.
100 bees, 100 birds,
This poem has 100 words!

Meish Goldish

Month-by-Month Poetry: December, January, February Scholastic Professional Books, 1999

To My Valentine

If apples were pears,
And peaches were plums,
And if the rose had a different name—
If tigers were bears,
And fingers were thumbs,
I'd love you just the same!

Anonymous

My Love Is Like a Cabbage

My love is like a cabbage
    Divided into two,
The leaves I give to others
    but the heart I give to you.

Traditional, English

Roses Are Red

Roses are red
Violets are blue
Carnations are sweet
And so are you.
And so are they
That send you this
And when we meet
We'll have a kiss.

Traditional, English

Month-by-Month Poetry: December, January, February   Scholastic Professional Books, 1999

Red Velvet Cats:
A Jump Rope Rhyme

Red-velvet cats and lace eared hounds...
Sam loves *Meg*
Or the other way around.
When *he* sees *her*,
His heart begins to pound.
Ribbons and roses and someone sweet...
How fast a second does *his* heart beat?
One, two, three, four, five, six...

Isabel Joshlin Glaser

The Porcupine

A porcupine looks somewhat silly,
He also is extremely quilly
And if he shoots a quill at you
Run fast
Or you'll be quilly too.

I would not want a porcupine
To be my loving valentine.

Karla Kuskin

I Love You

I love you,
I love you,
I love you
    so well,
If I had a
    peanut,
I'd give you
    the shell.

Anonymous

Presidents' Day

Remembering
what came before,
we raise old flags
in peace, in war.

Remembering
their names, their birth—
we fuse stone monuments
to earth.

Remembering
the brave, the great,
we mark these days
to celebrate.

Remembering
that we are free—
we write their lives
in history.

Myra Cohn Livingston

George Washington

CHORUS:
George, George Washington,
You're, you're number one!
George, George Washington,
You're number one to me!

Leader of the army,
An able general, George.
Strongly and bravely,
You led at Valley Forge!

CHORUS

Father of our country,
Our first President.
Proudly and wisely,
You led the government!

CHORUS

We celebrate your birthday,
Our capital has your name.
Your picture's on a dollar bill,
So all will know your fame!

CHORUS

You never told a lie, George,
You were brave and smart.
First in honor, first in peace,
First in our heart!

CHORUS

Meish Goldish

Month-by-Month Poetry: December, January, February Scholastic Professional Books, 1999

Lincoln

There was a boy of other days,
A quiet, awkward, earnest lad,
Who trudged long weary miles to get
A book on which his heart was set—
And then no candle had!

He was too poor to buy a lamp
But very wise in woodmen's ways.
He gathered seasoned bough and stem,
And crisping leaf, and kindled them
Into a ruddy blaze.

Then as he lay full length and read,
The firelight flickered on his face,
And etched his shadow on the gloom,
And made a picture in the room,
In that most humble place.

The hard years came, the hard years went,
But, gentle, brave, and strong of will,
He met them all. And when today
We see his pictured face, we say,
"There's light upon it still."

Nancy Byrd Turner

Slush Song

O I love to march through the mush
When the snow melts down into slush
My boots go SLIP-SLAP PLIT-PLAT SPLIT-SPLAT
Through the slickery sloggery slush!

O I'm not in a bit of a rush
When I'm out in the sloopery slush
I sloosh
And I slosh
And I splashily splosh
In the sliggery slubbery slush!

MUSH! MUSH! HUSH! HUSH! SLUSH! SLUSH!

O the slippery
  slobbery
   sluggery
    sloggery
     shushily
      mushily
       SLUSH!

Patricia Hubbell

Leap Year Lament

Leaping spiders
Leaping goats
"Leaping Lizards!"
   Too.
I'll play Leapfrog
'til I croak, but Leaping
birthdays will not
   Do!
My friend, Alicia's
eight years old while
I'm just turning
   TWO.

Pass the ice cream
Pass the hats
Pass the presents
   Please!
When Alicia's
twelve years old,
I'll be turning
   THREE.

Light those candles
Cut that cake
Sing to me once
   More!
For when Alicia's
"sweet sixteen"
I'll just be turning
   FOUR
      !

Jacqueline Sweeney

Rain

Summer rain
   is soft and cool,
   so I go barefoot
   in a pool.
But winter rain
   is cold, and pours,
   so I must watch it
   from indoors.

Myra Cohn Livingston

Month-by-Month Poetry: December, January, February Scholastic Professional Books, 1999

When Skies Are Low and Days Are Dark

When skies are low
and days are dark,
and frost bites
like a hungry shark,
when mufflers muffle
ears and nose,
and puffy sparrows
huddle close—
how nice to know
that February
is something purely
temporary.

N. M. Bodecker

The Bears Wake Up

When bears wake up
from hibernation
it's the time
for celebration.
No more sleeping
in the cold
while the snow
and ice grow cold.

Hibernation
dreams are done.
Time for really having fun.
Time for eating
everything,
time for feeling sunny spring.

Sandra Liatsos

Good-by My Winter Suit

Good-by my winter suit,
good-by my hat and boot,
good-by my ear-protecting muffs
and storms that hail and hoot.

Farewell to snow and sleet,
farewell to Cream of Wheat,
farewell to ice-removing salt
and slush around my feet.

Right on! to daffodils,
right on! to whippoorwills,
right on! to chirp-producing eggs
and baby birds and quills.

The day is on the wing,
the kite is on the string,
the sun is where the sun should be—
it's spring all right! It's spring!

N. M. Bodecker

Notes

Month-by-Month Poetry: December, January, February Scholastic Professional Books, 1999